# Baptism
## A thought for each day of the year

Philip M. Hudson

Copyright 2019 by Philip M. Hudson.

Published 2019.

Printed in the United States of America.

All rights reserved.

No portion of this book may be reproduced, stored in a retrieval system, or transmitted in any form or by any means – electronic, mechanical, photocopy, recording, scanning, or other – except for brief quotations in critical reviews or articles, without the prior written permission of the author.

ISBN 978-1-950647-22-4

Illustrations – Google Images.

This book may be ordered from online bookstores.

Publishing Services by BookCrafters
Parker, Colorado.
www.bookcrafters.net

# Table of Contents

Acknowledgements..................................................................................................i
Preface....................................................................................................................v
Introduction.........................................................................................................vii

A Thought For Each Day Of The Year..................................................................1
About The Author...............................................................................................367
By The Author....................................................................................................369
What More Can I Say?.......................................................................................373

Baptism
has purpose
and meaning
only for those
who are willing
to sacrifice their
broken heart and
contrite spirit to
the Savior of
the world.

# Acknowledgements

In this volume, I have attributed quotations to original authors whenever possible, as well as when I have editorialized their ideas. In many cases, however, my language will naturally reflect the teachings of leaders and members of The Church of Jesus Christ of Latter-day Saints.

The list of those who have contributed to this book is endless. As I have organized my own thoughts, I have realized how heavily I have borrowed from the towering examples of those who, over the years, have been my mystical mentors, my sensible chaperones, my spiritual guides, my surrogate saviors, my compassionate critics, and everything in between.

They are my avatars, manifestations of deity in bodily forms, my na'vi, the visionaries, who communicate with God on a level to which I can only aspire, and my tsaddik, whom I esteem as intuitive interpreters of biblical law and scripture. They are my divine teachers incarnate. They have offered listening ears, extended open arms, lifted my spirits, shown me the way, stretched my mind, reinforced my faith, strengthened my testimony, helped me to discover my wings, given immaterial support, provided of their means, emboldened me with words of encouragement, cheered me on with wise counsel, taught me humility, been there to steady me, soothed my troubled soul, stepped in to nurture me, led me to fountains of living water, wet my parched lips with inspired counsel, and bound up my wounds.

When I think of the influence of a multitude of angels thinly disguised as my family, friends, and peers, I remember the words of Sir Isaac Newton, who, when pressed to reveal the great secret behind his accomplishments, simply replied: "I stood on the shoulders of giants." Of course, at the end of the day, I alone am responsible for the content of this volume. But I hope my interpretations of principles and doctrine will cultivate your interest to dig deeper into the themes woven into this tapestry, by turning to the scriptures and seeking inspiration from the Spirit. My only goal is to help you to expand your insights into the telestial mile markers, the terrestrial truths, and the celestial guidelines that accompany each of us during our quest for enlightenment through baptism.

The elements
of baptism speak
to our spirits, for every
Gospel principle carries within
itself a witness that it is true. Its
language is universal, and when our
minds have been illuminated by faith,
we enjoy fluency, familiarity, and an
easy comfort with the revealed word
of God that opens up vistas of
eternal proportion before
our eyes.

It is baptism that
captures the heart of a little
child before it has been exposed to
the cankering influence and corrosive
elements of the world, before their hearts
are set upon temporal things, and their
spirituality has been so weakened that
the things of God are no longer part
of their daily experience. Better than
the rest of us, little children have a
capacity to "lay aside the things
of this world, and seek for
the things of a better."
(D&C 25:10).

# Preface

I love to learn by reading the scriptures, and I often think of St. Hilary, who wrote in the third century: "Scripture consists not in what we read, but in what we understand." In each of the musings within this volume, I have consistently tried to find a scriptural foundation and a spiritual confirmation as I put my pen to paper.

I am continually reminded of Nephi's counsel to press forward with complete dedication and steadfastness, or confidence with a firm determination in Christ, having a perfect brightness of hope, or perfect faith, and charity, or a love of God and of all men. If we do this, feasting upon the word of Christ, or receiving strength and nourishment as we ponder the doctrines of the kingdom, and particularly the doctrine of baptism, and as we then endure to the end in righteousness, we shall have eternal life, which is the greatest of God's gifts. (See 2 Nephi 31:20).

It is with love, then, that I extend to you the invitation to enjoy this omnibus of random thoughts. Embrace it at face value, and use its observations relating to baptism as a springboard to your own personal plateaus of discovery, as you are taught by the Spirit to move in the direction of your dreams.

Ultimately, we are required to give up only our sins, that we might merit salvation thru baptism by the grace of God.

# Introduction

If they are fortunate, novice quilters quickly learn a bit of wisdom from the Amish, who make some of the finest quilts in the world. On purpose, the Amish build mistakes into their projects, because they believe that any attempt on their part to design and produce a flawless creation would be a mockery of God, Who alone is perfect. The humility of the Amish makes me think of my own weak attempts to put the thoughts expressed in this omnibus to paper. In His infinite wisdom, God knows very well that I do not need to consciously plan on lacing my efforts with errors. That will come quite naturally, without the need for me to intentionally contribute to my short-comings.

Perhaps this serendipitous collection of musings will do little more than help to define quirks in my personality. Each of us is different, and many things, including our family and friends, the circumstances in which we find ourselves, the quality of our education, and our own personalities, inspire and mold our oral and written expressions. I would like to think that, in this text, all of these influences have been encouraging, affirmative, and constructive.

The reflections within this tome leave the door ajar for the reader, to allow shafts of the light of understanding to creep in. If, as I have expressed my thoughts, I mis-stated myself a few times, or flat-out got it wrong, I ask the patient indulgence and gentle correction of the reader.

Too often, I realize that my communications can be "carefully disguised with hypocrisy and glittering words," as Einstein put it. Although I do fancy myself a wordsmith, I have tried to avoid pedestrian expressions, idle language, and lazy scholarship. I do not pretend to be an authority on the doctrine of baptism, inasmuch as I believe that we are all works in progress, but if you find the factual tone of a particular musing disengaging, the truth is that I typically experienced a deep personal involvement in my interpretation of the principles that illuminated its meaning.

In any event, when you open this volume, I hope you ponder these minute musings with as much enjoyment as I have experienced while creating them.

We are baptized
that we might be better
prepared to travel the path
that leads to the Kingdom of
God. We await the further light
and knowledge He has promised
to send to us through
His prophets.

The Holy Ghost
invites us to be baptized,
that we might thereafter enjoy
the quiet serenity of the Sabbath
day as we never have before. We are
introduced to new experiences during
a day of worship, service, and rest
that take us away from the tumult
of the teeming multitudes that
often characterizes the lives
of those who have not
yet entered the
fold.

We are baptized
to vitalize the Plan
of Happiness. Baptism
provides insight into the
spiritual roots that are at the
foundation of relationships that
are themselves the products of our
interconnectivity and interdependence.

The Hubble
telescope can
"see" 13.2 billion
light years into our
past, almost back to the
moment of creation itself,
but it cannot gaze into the
heavens for five minutes.
Only a baptismal service
can do that.

We are baptized "through the infinite goodness of God, (that by) the manifestations of his Spirit (we might) have great views of that which is to come." (Mosiah 5:3). Rather than multiplying mirrors by studying angles without increasing the light, baptism illuminates our minds by the Spirit.

When we
are baptized
we are blessed
with the courage
to be "witnesses of
God at all times and
in all things, and in all
places." (Mosiah 18:9).

Our baptism proclaims tidings of great joy, and carries us on a groundswell of emotion that lifts us heavenward. Worship is elevated to something more dynamic than the simple mechanical observance of a multiplicity of ceremonial rules. Publishing peace is the daily antidote to worldly tendencies that canker our souls.

We are baptized that we might reconnect with our spiritual Birth Parents, for we are the sons and daughters of "the living God." (Hosea 1:10). "The Spirit itself beareth witness with our spirit, that we are the children of God." (Romans 8:16). We find answers to our yearning to know: "Have we not all one father?" We ask the question: "Hath not one God created us?" (Malachi 2:10).

We are baptized
that Heavenly Father
might create in our behalf
an impenetrable shield of faith
in our Lord Jesus Christ. Each of
us has been fitted with protection that
has been tailored to our unique and
distinctive needs. Its elements are
strengthened by the covenants
we make with Him.

We are baptized that opposition might become a blessing that allows us to fully engage The Plan of God.

The path that lies
beyond the baptismal font
leads to the Tree of Life. It
is not a freeway, but is a toll
road. Until we have paid its price,
we cannot hope to comprehend with
fluency the language of the Spirit
that explains how to make our
way to the tree, that we might
harvest its delicious fruit.

When
we step out
of the baptismal
font, our faces are
oriented toward the
light. However, as our
knowledge grows, so do
the borders of darkness
that encroach upon the
edge of the light. The
more we know, the
more we realize
how much we
have to
learn.

Our baptism
blesses us with
the tools we need
to calibrate our lives
with the pattern of heaven
itself. Because we have come
from the eternal vantage point
of the abode of the Gods, a
resetting of our celestial
chronometer to a more
easily recognizable
temporal scale is
required.

Baptism
blesses us with
a currency of faith
that accrues with interest.
As we quietly carry out our
work as disciples of Christ, the
righteousness of our cause is
revealed to us in simplicity
and plainness. Barriers to
our personal progress
crumble and fall
away.

We
were baptized
that we might learn
how to consecrate to
the Lord our time, our
talents, our means, and
all else with which He
has providently
blessed our
lives.

After we
have been baptized,
we have little inclination
to look back, as we flee from
Sodom and Gomorrah. We leave
the ranks of those who have nestled
themselves into a vacation retreat
in Babylon, even though their
home address is in Zion.

We are baptized
that, henceforth, we
be no longer carried
about with every wind of
doctrine, which are those
worldly influences that
play mind-games with
us, as they jockey
for position in a
competition for
market share.

Our
baptism compels
us to consider the
possibility that we might
one day be like the Savior.
We believe that His grace consists
of the gifts and power by which we
may be brought to His perfection
and stature, so that we may
enjoy not only what
He has, but also
what He
is.

Those who
demand outward
evidence of the power
of God as a condition of
their belief seek to circumvent
the process by which both faith and
knowledge are developed. They want
the proof, but without having first paid
the price. As with adulterers, who expect
immediate gratification, they want to be
theologically titillation by experiencing
the result, but without having first
accepted the responsibility.

Baptism
blesses us to be
able to reach out
and touch the face of
God with an incorruptible
and unimpeachable spiritual
sixth sense that finds its
expression deep inside
us, within our own
hearts.

We have an abiding faith
in the promise that, because
of our baptismal covenant, one
day in the not too distant future
the atmosphere that we breathe will
be pungent with a heavenly aether that
is punctuated by the melodious strains of
our native tongue. Every detail will be
just as we had imagined it would be,
including the reassuring radiant
heat of a celestial fire that has
been kindled beforehand by
Father, in preparation for
our homecoming.

At our baptism, we are given an extra measure of resolve to see life through to its end. When our challenges seem overwhelming, our covenants stand ready to offer assistance related to their resolution.

We
are baptized to
evenly distribute the
weight of our temporal
baggage, that it might
be easier for us to
enter in at the
strait gate.

We are baptized that we might have hope in our Savior. It invites us to consider the possibility that we might one day be like Him. We believe that His grace consists of the gifts and power by which we may be brought to His perfection and stature, so that we may enjoy not only what He has, but also what He is.

We are baptized that we might speak "the truth in love, (and) grow up into him in all things, which is the head, even Christ." (Ephesians 4:15).

God has
prepared baptism
as our ticket to a work
release program, that has
been designed to see just how
we would behave when left on
our own, after having received
unambiguous instruction from
above, relating to what we
ought to be doing with
the time that has been
allotted to each
of us.

We are baptized that the Spirit of the Lord Omnipotent might work "a mighty change in us, or in our hearts, that we have no more disposition to do evil, but to do good continually." (Mosiah 5:2).

It is our baptism that knits our hearts together in unity and in love. It is the first of several steps that give those who are living on both sides of the veil the tools they need to successfully confront eternity.

As we prepare ourselves to be baptized, angels will attend us. "For I will go before your face," promised the Savior. "I will be on your right hand, and on your left, and my Spirit shall be in your hearts, and mine angels round about you, to bear you up." (D&C 84:88). With such a promise, how could we think to turn our backs on this reinforcement, return to our wicked ways, and go it alone?

Timid souls who are cautiously hesitant and tentatively faithful don't consciously intend to ignore the spiritual prompting that urges them to to be baptized. Their desire just fades away, like the slow leak in an bicycle tire, and not as a blowout.

We are baptized
that we might know
that we are here, at this
time, and in this place, by
divine design. What we think
are merely coincidences, when
they are viewed thru the clarifying
lens of baptism, are faith promoting
examples of the Lord patiently working
behind the scenes in our behalf. Nothing
in this life happens by chance. Everything
that is of significance happens by
divine approbation.

Baptism
emancipates us from
the self-limiting conditions
that had heretofore blinded us
to a larger view of life. It frees us to
pay closer attention to celestial guideposts
and principles. It invites us to experience more
intense and reflective self-awareness, deeper
and more abiding humility, reinvigorated
confidence, and incomprehensively
more profound and
enduring faith.

"This is the
Gospel which I have given
unto you - that I came into the
world to do the will of my Father,
because my Father sent me ... And
it shall come to pass, that whoso
repenteth and is baptized in
my name shall be filled."
(3 Nephi 27:13-20).

The essential key to our liberation from the bondage to sin, which is our freedom to become, is an adjustment in attitude that is reflected in our desire to be washed clean in the shining waters of purification. Paraphrasing Helen Keller, the real tragedy is not those of us who are born without sight, but those of us who have our sight, but who do not have vision.

We are baptized when we have determined to follow the Savior "with full purpose of heart, acting no hypocrisy and no deception before God." (2 Nephi 31:13). When we do so, the night of darkness will be followed by a Renaissance, a spiritual rebirth that paves the way for our enlightenment. Our world will blossom with new ideas and unbridled optimism, for is we of whom Isaiah spoke. Although we walked in darkness, we have now seen a great light. We dwell in the land of the shadow of death, but now, the Holy Ghost shines upon us. (See Isaiah 9:2).

When
Adam and
Eve were driven
from the Garden,
they were "punished"
with the very thing that
would later prove to bring
them the greatest happiness. As
the Sufi poet Rumi observed, our
wounds become portals that allow
light to enter us. A Savior would be
provided for them, but in the interim,
cherubim and a flaming sword were
placed to keep the way of the Tree
of Life, to honor the doctrines of
Justice and Mercy, as well as
the principle of repentance,
that they had been taught
in consequence of
transgression.

The cataracts that are created by our concessions to sin cloud our vision. Our narrow perspective forces us into making comfortless compromises, leaving the landscapes of our lives as nothing more than empty shells. If we do not take advantage of the therapy of baptism, the prognosis is poor for eyes that have lost the ability to see clearly, and that can no longer make the distinctions between good and evil, and between light and darkness.

The
raw and ugly
contamination of sin
is incompatible with the
uncompromising standard of
spiritual hygiene that is required
of those who have been baptized
who, one day, hope to be able
to inhabit heaven and live
in the company of God
and angels.

The
Apostle
Paul observed
of the Athenians,
who were not so very
different from many in
our day, that they bowed down
before unknown gods, whom they
ignorantly worshipped. It is in the
hope that we might be able to stand
independently in our witness of
Jesus Christ, Who is the true
and living God, that we
are baptized.

At our baptism,
we consecrate our
lives to the Savior. We
cast ourselves on an altar
of faith whose foundation is
buttressed by a supernal display
of divine direction. We are driven
forward by unwavering confidence
that His power to save might be
unleashed in our behalf and
flow over our wounds as a
healing balm, so that we
might be able to meet
His penetrating gaze
with unencumbered
hearts and clear
eyes.

Perfect obedience to laws
and ordinances qualifies us
to enter into the Rest of the Lord.
It has the power to move us along the
path to the point that we reflect God's
divine nature and feel comfortable in
the presence of the Spirit. This is one
of the reasons why we repetitively
renew our baptismal covenant
in the Sacrament, and why
we frequently rehearse
the veil experience
in the temple.

When we
are baptized,
the anchors of
our faith rest upon
a foundation of rock,
rather than of sand. Our
testimonies are composed of
three essential elements. First
is our conscious recognition of
Gospel principles. Second is our
understanding of the Lord's word
concerning the principles. Finally,
is our direct experience with the
principles, which we call the
fruits of faith.

Our baptisms
open our hearts
and our minds to a
breathtaking expansion
of understanding. As we
practice a learning style
that embraces the Spirit,
we discover the pattern
of heaven, and it
becomes our
norm.

Wherever and
whenever a disciple
of Christ has been baptized
by immersion for the remission
of their sins, and each time the gift
of the Holy Ghost falls upon another
investigator of truth, the future looks
brighter, because the advancing tide of
wickedness will have slowed down just
a bit. A thousand points of light, when
gathered together in one from every
corner of the globe, will cast, in
every direction, a very long
shadow of influence.

With our
baptisms, our attention
is focused on our faith, and the
covenant encourages us to nurture
it in many ways. Every day thereafter,
we take our testimony temperature,
and hope to regularly detect
its feverish pitch.

Baptism
and the gift of
the Holy Ghost, are
the "fruit of the Spirit"
that we receive when we
have been taught the
doctrine of Christ.
(Galatians 5:22).

With baptism,
there comes a familiarity
with principles that stands in sharp
contrast to the values of society that are
continually morphed by the shifting sands of
cultural expediency. The covenants we make at
baptism protect us from these mutating
standards, and provide a stable
moral basis that shapes us as
we develop into the full
stature of our spirits.

When we are baptized,
we affirm the innocence of
little children. It was an integral
element of The Plan that was ordained
in the Grand Council in Heaven before the
world was, that little ones who died before
reaching the age of accountability would
be saved in the Kingdom of God by the
power of the Atonement. They are
blameless from the beginning.

When we
have been spiritually
begotten of Christ, we are
given the invitation to re-write
the record of our lives. We cannot
go back and start a new beginning,
but we can begin now to make
a new ending. Our lives can
become fairytales that
are waiting to
be written.

We are baptized that we might hear the voice of the Lord that is unto all, for "there is none to escape; and there is no eye that shall not see, neither ear that shall not hear, neither heart that shall not be penetrated." (D&C 1:2).

Baptism prepares us
to move onward along
a steady course of progress
without encumbering ourselves
with the wobbly constraints of
uncertainty that always lie in
wait to mislead those who
manifest a timid and
hesitant spiritual
constitution.

We submit to
baptism that, with
our hands uplifted
unto the Most High,
our incomings, our
outgoings, and our
salutations might
be in the name
of the Lord.

The pathway to
heaven is illuminated by the
principles of conversion that point
us in the direction of our recognition
of our iniquity and then to a deep godly
sorrow for our sins. Next comes inescapable
suffering and torment that stimulates an
appeal to the Savior, with an awakening
understanding of the Atonement. With
our baptism, comes the remission of
our sins, spiritual enlightenment,
and great joy. This motivates
us to embrace a lifestyle of
righteousness and service.
Each time this happens,
the loop cycles one
more time, but it is
calibrated toward
a higher plane
of existence.

To paraphrase the Apostle Paul: Thanks be to God that our baptism gives us the opportunity to lead quiet and peaceful lives in all godliness and honesty.

When our faith has finally
convicted us of our sins, and we
approach the font, we bow our heads
in reverence. The words of the baptismal
prayer orient our thoughts on the stars, and
even lift them to eternity, no matter where we
may have been bobbing about on the vast ocean
of life. Initially, getting a fix on its symbolism
that comes alive with intentional imagery and
magical metaphor might seem daunting. But
soon, timeless messages that are conveyed
by the Spirit, and have come down to us
from the wide expanse of heaven will
transcend time and loom larger
than life itself.

Baptism
was carefully
crafted to create
the conditions wherein
we might be prompted and
strengthened by the Light of
Christ and the Holy Ghost to
choose the harder right, and
in faith, make the most of
the cradle and crucible
of our experience.

No
wind can
blow except
it fills our sails to
carry each of us ever
closer to our destination,
without delay or interruption,
and without unnecessary cost,
loss, or sacrifice. The only
requirement for baptism
is the sacrifice of a
broken heart and
contrite spirit.

With our
baptism, we feel the word
enlarge our souls and enlighten
our understanding. As Brigham Young
said: "Every Gospel principle carries within
it a witness that it is true." In the economy of
the Gospel, "we often catch a spark from the
awakened memories of the immortal soul,
which lights up our whole being as with
the glory of our former home."
(Joseph F. Smith).

Our baptism
gives us the opportunity
to literally have the best of
both worlds; to live on earth,
but still enjoy a heavenly
peace that surpasses
understanding.

Baptism is
the first definitive step
on our journey to Christ. The path
that lies beyond the font leads to the
tree of life. It is not a freeway, but a
toll road. Until we have paid the price,
we cannot hope to comprehend with
fluency the language of the Spirit
that clearly explains how to
make our way to the tree,
that we might harvest
its delicious fruit.

Our covenant of
baptism quickens us
to use opposition as the
tool it was intended to be;
to open up a portal to the Spirit
Who will then empower us to do all
things that are expedient in His sight.
At that point, we have an epiphany,
when we are at-one with the
mind and will of God.

No matter that we
may live in the frigid
reaches of the Arctic or in
the stifling heat of the tropics.
It is in the invigorating waters of
baptism that we catch a religious fever
that elevates our testimony temperature
enough to get our juices flowing with an
appreciation of Who the Savior really is. It
is at this moment that we prepare ourselves
to experience the earth shaking and mind
bending theophany that we who once were
the children of men, have become His
spiritual offspring. We are born
of Him Who lives in heaven
on the right hand of the
throne of God.

Baptism is the
temporal witness
of a Gospel principle
that is eternally valid.
Baptism is more than the
expression of values, which
are beliefs that are culturally
or personally determined
and may change with
circumstances.

We are baptized
that we might learn
to abide by the laws of
heaven, even as we tarry
upon the earth. We yearn for
our hearts to burn within us,
as the Spirit speaks with us
and opens the scriptures
to our understanding.

Temporal
baggage can
create imbalance
that leads to confusion.
Baptism jars us out of our
collective complacency by upsetting
the stagnation of the status quo. It invites
us to enjoy a settled conviction in our minds
by getting our juices flowing, prodding us to
constructively expend our energy, and
putting our agency to work.

After our baptism,
we return to the real
world, to be sent forth as
sheep in the midst of wolves.
However, we are provided a shield
of protection against the spatter of
corrosive perspiration cast off by the
destroyer, who, we learn, will work
overtime to damage our doctrinal
defenses, diminish our charitable
capacity, deplete our bountiful
reservoirs of sympathy, dull
our spiritual sensitivities,
and destroy our
devotions.

Whether we are
professional athletes
or practiced panhandlers,
living in the fast or the slow
lane of life, whether we have rags
or riches, are leaders or lepers, are
early prodigies or late bloomers, venture
capitalists or welfare recipients; no matter
what our circumstances may be, our baptism
builds a bridge over the troubled waters
of faltering faith. We move beyond the
yellow brick road that leads only
to Oz, to the strait and narrow
path that will guide us to the
gate of heaven itself.

At our baptism,
when our souls have
been illuminated by the
burning Spirit of God, we
can no longer remain passive.
The flickering fire of faith warms
our souls as we begin to recognize the
upward reach within ourselves. We are
sensitized to truth and beauty, and to
a goodness above and beyond our
own attainment. We experience
the unmistakable stirrings
of gratitude from deep
within our hearts.

Baptism lights
a candle instead
of cursing the
darkness.

With baptism, we choose liberty and eternal life, instead of captivity and spiritual death. We choose to live our lives within the framework of the Gospel and its laws. Without it, unbridled freedom would lead to tyranny. We are free to choose whether or not we wish to be baptized, but we cannot choose to escape the consequences, should we choose unwisely.

The differences
between us matter very little.
Saints and sinners are not so very
different, after all. Baptism
is the great equalizer.
(See Acts 10:34).

Baptism was not
conceived to follow the
receipt of signs from heaven.
Our faith precedes the miracle.
We must take a few steps into the
darkness, and then faith, that spiritual
strong searchlight, will illuminate
the way. Spiritual confirmation
always flows along the
pathway created
by faith.

A
conduit
to living water
is created when we not
only believe, but also act on
our belief, by being honest, true,
chaste, benevolent, virtuous, kind,
and in doing good to others.

When we are baptized, we are inspired to enjoy feelings of serenity and harmony, in ways that were thoughtfully programmed by our Heavenly Father to touch our heart strings.

We are
baptized to
facilitate both the
temporal and spiritual
execution of The Plan. Our
baptismal covenant allows us to
continually monitor our relationship
with God during our engagement with
mortality. Our salvation hinges upon our
correct understanding of the points of
doctrine that focus on salvation.

We are
introduced thru
baptism to the Holy
Ghost, Who is the author
of our acumen, the avatar
of our agency, the architect
of our aptitude, the benefactor of
all of our blessings, the designer of
our discipleship, the initiator of insight,
the inventor of intelligence, the patron
of perception, the provider of praise,
the sponsor of scholarship, and the
ultimate source of understanding;
as well as the craftsman of our
comfort, the guarantor of all
gifts, and the champion of
committed Christians
everywhere.

We are baptized
that we might be given
the tools we need in order
to lengthen our stride. In a
confrontation of principles with
values, that tears at the fabric of
the natural world, the Savior asks
us to exert ourselves with actions
that will stretch the limits of our
abilities. But in the process, we
will find the Source of our
untapped spiritual
strength.

In Ephesians 4:13
we read that we are
baptized that we might
"come in the unity of the
faith, and of the knowledge
of the Son of God ... unto the
... stature of the fulness of Christ."
We retain our distinct individuality
as the spirt-born sons and daughters
of God, but we become unified in
every other way.

Baptism helps us to appreciate how all three members of the Godhead work in our behalf to provide the blessing of immortality and eternal life. "For by the water (we) keep the commandment; by the Spirit (we) are justified, and by the blood (we) are sanctified."
(Moses 6:60).

We are baptized
because we want to
"be redeemed of God,
and (to) be numbered with
those of the first resurrection,
that (we might) have eternal
life." (Mosiah 18:9).

Our baptism activates
the redemption exemption
that is a codicil to the Law
of Justice, as our lease on
life is renegotiated to
our advantage.

It seems
indisputable that
the object and design
of our existence, following
our baptism for the remission
of our sins, would be to become
the happiest people upon the face
of the earth. Our obedience must
unleash a spiritual cornucopia.
We feast upon the nourishing
bread of life that has been
provided, and drink from
a well of living water.
Life could not be
better!

When we
are baptized
we become as lights
that are set on a hill. We
build up our discipleship with
dignity and make it honorable
and enlarge and strengthen it.
We simply perform the service
that pertains to it.

We are baptized because
none of us would choose to become
spiritually depleted, or to perish because
we neglect the things that matter most. We
understand the consequences of spiritual
starvation, doctrinal dehydration,
and intellectual inhibition.

Following our baptism, we
discover that obedience is no longer
inconvenient, but has become our quest.
In that moment, said Ezra Taft Benson, God
endows us with power. When we are diligent in
our obedience, our agency enjoys its
greatest expression. This is one
of the hardest things for
the unconverted to
understand.

On that special day, when we step down into the font and are immersed in the waters of baptism, we figuratively and literally bow our knees "unto the Father of our Lord Jesus Christ, of whom the whole family in heaven and earth is named." (Ephesians 3:14-15).

If we
ignore the
influences of
the Light of Christ
and the Holy Ghost that
support our innate urge to
follow the spiritual prompting
to be baptized, but instead allow
ourselves to be distracted by trifling
concerns, we sin by omission and risk
settling for life in a marshland of
mediocrity that can mutate into
a quicksand of sin, from
which there will be
no easy escape.

Our faith
notwithstanding,
we are saved by the
grace of God, after all
we can do, and that is
primarily to repent
and be baptized.

Our baptism will
bind us to heaven by
creating a pulsing stream
of inspiration whose flow has
has no temporal boundary and
no spatial limitation. We will
find that we are one with
the mind and will
of God.

Unlike the
repentant, who
approach the waters
of baptism in humility,
those who are proud are
more comfortable with their
own perception of truth than
they are with God's omniscience.
They pit their own abilities against
His priesthood power, their own
paltry overtures against His
mighty works, and their
stubborn won't against
His gentle will.

Pride is motivated by self-will, while baptism is inspired by God's will. Pride is driven by the fear of man, while baptism is nurtured by the love of God. The applause of the world rings loudly in the ears of the prideful, but it is the accolades of heaven that warm the hearts of the repentant faithful.

Those who
decline the offer of
the riches of eternity that
might have been unfolded to
their view through the power of
the Atonement and the ordinance
of baptism for the remission of sin,
are doomed to live out their lives
in scarcity of their basic spiritual
needs. They live beneath the
poverty level, and may
not even be aware
of it.

We are "baptized after the manner of his burial, being buried in the water in his name, and this according to the commandment which he has given – That by keeping the commandments (we) might be washed and cleansed from all (our) sins."
(D&C 76:51-52).

At our baptism, if we listen
very carefully, we can hear the
gentle rustling of the wings of angels
coming from behind a slightly-parted veil.
The company of beings from the unseen
world sweeps the cobwebs from our
minds and opens up to our view
undreamed vistas of otherwise
inaccessible experience.

It is only after our baptism that we will be given the tools we will need to experience God's Rest. As we wend our way through this vale of tears, the real journey to Christ has only just begun. When we are born again in our baptism, we lay aside those sins which had besought us, threatening to bring us down to destruction, for the promise of a better and more enduring substance.

After our baptism,
we enjoy the influence
of the Holy Ghost, which
teaches the peaceable things
of the kingdom. We matriculate
into a curriculum where we learn
to understand with fluency the
language of the Spirit.

The world's definition of peace is remarkably superficial. Often-times, peace is only equated with the lack of bloodshed or active combatants. The Lord's definition is quite different. "His peace is not the peace of the world of ease, of luxury, idleness, absence of turmoil and strife, but the peace born of the righteous life, the peace that lifts the soul, that day by day brings us closer to the home of Eternal Peace, the dwelling place of our Father." (J. Reuben Clark, Jr.).

Baptism speaks
to our spirits, for every
Gospel principle carries within
itself a witness that it is true. Its
language is universal, and when the
Holy Ghost illuminates our minds, we
enjoy fluency, familiarity, and ease
with the doctrines, and comfort
with the revealed word of
God that opens up vistas
of eternal proportion
before our eyes.

Our covenant of baptism has been designed to make saints of sinners as it works on us to hate our former lives in the world, and to strive to be better than we have ever been before, by finding ways to minister to the needs of others. It pushes us out of our comfort zones that can be suffocating to our spirits.

We are baptized "that we henceforth be no more children, tossed to and fro." (Ephesians 4:14). Our baptismal covenant is God's promise that He will never leave us to fight our battles alone.

We are
baptized with
a promise that
we might become
kings and priests, and
queens and priestesses; in
sum to become rightful
heirs of the blessings
that belonged to
the fathers.

Those who follow the example of the Savior, Who was baptized to fulfil all righteousness, and approach the waters of baptism "in obedience to the commandments, shall receive health in their navel and marrow to their bones; and shall find wisdom and great treasures of knowledge, even hidden treasures; and shall run and not be weary, and shall walk and not faint." (D&C 89:18).

As we
quietly prepare
for baptism, the
righteousness of our
efforts will be revealed
in spectacular simplicity
and plainness. The walls of
opposition to our purposeful
repentance will crumble and
fall away. In our efforts, the
Lord will comfort and succor
us with the bread of life. As we
journey through the harsh and
unforgiving environment of
mortality, seeking the Lord
while He may be found,
oases will spring up
in the desert and
living water will
slake our
thirst.

Baptism may be a hard principle for us to grasp because it was conceived in heaven. It is not of this world, and so if we try to wrap our finite minds around it, we will fail to do so. It is spiritually discerned.

Baptism can catalyze our relationship with God, when it unshackles us from the icy grip of our captivity to Satan; and all is because of the Atonement of Christ.

Baptism is
just the prescription
the Doctor ordered to
treat the religious fever
that elevates our testimony
temperature enough to get
our juices flowing with
an appreciation of the
Savior's sacrifice.

The unblemished
innocence of our little ones
who are about to be baptized makes
us optimistic that peace is within our reach.
When we become as little children, "submissive,
meek, humble, patient, (and) full of love,"
the enticings of the Holy Spirit help us
to put off the natural man and
to become saints through the
Atonement of Jesus Christ.
(Mosiah 3:19).

When we
are baptized, we mark
the calendar, that we might
thereafter, and for all eternity,
commemorate the birthdate of
our immortal souls, the end
of our being, and the
commencement of
our becoming.

Our baptism
makes a modest
public statement about a
profound private conviction.
Every day thereafter, we take
our testimony temperature,
and hope to regularly
detect its feverish
pitch.

We are baptized because the distance to the Celestial Kingdom of God is measured in faith, and not miles. It is not a question of dollars and cents, but of commitment.

Baptism is
the fire fueling
our determination
to follow the Savior.
His Atonement charges
our spiritual batteries and
energize our vision with
infinite perspective.
We can be holy
and without
spot.

Baptism represents
more than the making
of resolutions, that can be
nothing more than promises
to ourselves that are generally
kept for just a few days or weeks,
before they are abandoned and we
return to our former lifestyles.
The ordinance of baptism has
staying power. Baptism has
no bias; its basis is belief,
nurtured by the culture
medium of faith, our
repentance and the
companionship
of the Spirit.

When we are
baptized, we are
pleasantly surprised
to discover that the Lord
is on our right, and on our
left, and in our hearts. We are
strengthened by a multitude of
angels thinly disguised as our
family and friends. We recall
the words of Sir Isaac Newton,
who, when he was pressed to
reveal the secret behind his
accomplishments, simply
replied: "I stood on the
shoulders of giants."

We are baptized in
a process of generation,
and not just of maturation.
Mortality has been designed to
be a lifelong learning laboratory
to give each of us the opportunity to
mold our nature so that it more closely
resembles that of our Father in Heaven.
He initiated baptism to make that
metamorphosis possible.

Baptism helps us to more easily memorize our lines in the Three Act Play that has a catchy title: It is the "Plan of Salvation."

At our baptismal services in particular, we feel the Spirit through the medium of music. We are reminded that even before the foundations of the earth were laid, music filled the celestial air, when "the morning stars sang together, and all the sons of God shouted for joy." (Job 38:7).

If we
want the knowledge
of the Lord to cover
the earth, we need to plan
our work, and work The Plan,
and to define our dreams so
that we may understand
beforehand the costs
required to meet
our goals.

Reflection can
be a good thing, especially
when the light of Christ shines on our
countenances. As Alma asked the people of
Zarahemla: "And now, behold, I ask of you,
my brethren of the church, have ye spiritually
been born of God? Have ye received His
image in your countenances? Have
ye experienced this mighty
change in your heart?"
(Alma 5:14).

"For if we have been planted together in the likeness of his death, we shall be also in the likeness of his resurrection. Knowing this, that our old man is crucified with him, that the body of sin might be destroyed, that henceforth we should not serve sin."
(Romans 6:5-6).

After our
baptism, the Holy Ghost
guides us to covenants relating
to the priesthood and the temple.
"I will give unto the children of men
line upon line, precept upon precept, here
a little and there a little; and blessed are
those who hearken unto my precepts, and
lend an ear unto my counsel, for they
shall learn wisdom; for unto him
that receiveth I will give more."
(2 Nephi 28:30).

We become the sons and daughters of God, even one in our Savior Jesus Christ, as He is one in the Father, and the Father one in Him, that we may be one. (See D&C 35:2). We retain our distinct individuality, but become unified in every other way.

Our baptism clothes
us in spiritual chain-mail,
as protection against the fiery
darts of the adversary. Although
telestial turf is Satan's home ground,
and the quicksand of secular humanism
and other false ideologies lies ready to
suck the unwary into the underworld
of Beelzebub, no power on earth or
hell can overthrow or defeat that
which God has decreed.

We are baptized
in a dramatic validation
of the influence of the Light
of Christ, and of the power of the
Holy Ghost. These influences will labor
among us "till we all come in the unity of
the faith, and of the knowledge of the Son of
God, unto a perfect man, unto the measure
of the stature of the fulness of Christ."
(Ephesians 4:13).

Our Heavenly Father has created a Plan that is all the more beautiful because of its simplicity. It is clearly established in the Bible but it has been clarified in its companion scriptures. It has been carefully articulated in both The Book of Mormon and the Doctrine and Covenants, in order to silence disputations among the people concerning this vital point of doctrine.

Baptism is possible because of the Atonement, which can save us from our natural state of carnality, sensuality, and devilish inclinations. It activates the Law of Mercy, which mitigates for those who conform to its requirements the effects of the first Law, that demands Justice. It lifts us to a state of holiness, spirituality, angelic innocence, and happiness. It prepares us to feel comfortable in our heavenly home, where we will find ourselves in the presence of angels softly singing celestial lullabies that express only love.

Agency and opposition are always before us, and our baptism stands as a sacred sentinel, beckoning us to enter in at heaven's gate, to find the Rest of God.

Our baptism,
and the Atonement of
Christ, make life eternal,
love immortal, and death
only a horizon, which is
nothing, save the limit
of our sight.

Habitual
sin is a quicksand
that mires the unwary in
a monotonously repetitive and
underwhelming convention, and
in a mind-numbing conformity.
These are the opposites of the
imaginative spontaneity and
the refreshingly distinctive
artistic individuality of
those who submit to
the ordinance of
baptism.

The arrogant, boastful, conceited, haughty, and self-centered nature of the proud is easily trumped by the altruistic, modest, meek, and deferential behavior of the repentant, whose firm grasp on the horns of sanctuary that is represented by baptism confirms their faith in the invincible power of God.

Moral discipline involves the consistent exercise of agency to embrace ennobling eternal principles with action that is simply the right thing to do, although it may not be easy or convenient. If we want to have positive outcomes, however, our God-given right to choose must be accompanied by the strength to exercise moral discipline in the face of opposition. That is precisely the behavior that leads to the waters of baptism.

If we repent, we never thirst, because we are anchored through Gospel topsoil into a fountain of living water. Baptism is the ultimate expression of honesty with ourselves, with Heavenly Father, with the Savior, and with the Holy Ghost.

Moses counseled the Israelites to build upon the Rock of their salvation. He urged them to "write (their covenants) upon the posts of (their) houses" and to "not appear before the Lord empty" handed. (Deuteronomy 6:9 & 16:16). We would do well to do likewise, by remembering our covenant of baptism to take His name upon ourselves, that we might keep his commandments, and always remember Him.

Pride asks: "What do I want out of life?" but baptism meekly inquires: "What would God have me do?"

The Manual of Discipline that was written upon The Serek Scroll at Qumran vividly describes the rebirth that follows our baptism: "Our sins are forgiven us, and in the humility of our soul we are for all the Laws of God; our flesh is cleansed shining bright in the waters of purification, even in the waters of baptism, and we shall be given a new name in due time to walk perfectly in all the ways of God."

We are baptized
that we might be given
the tools to burst free of
our self-imposed limitations.
The powers of heaven and earth
amplify each other, and carry
us along on waves of
the Spirit.

With our baptism, we are liberated from self defeating behaviors. Obedience to Gospel principles blesses us to "be like the bird who, pausing in her flight awhile on boughs too light, feels them give way beneath her, and yet sings, knowing she hath wings." (Victor Hugo).

We are baptized that we might "be full of the knowledge of the Lord, as the waters cover the sea." (Isaiah 11:9). Our baptism leaves the world a better place than it was before we found our faith, and the truth.

We are baptized
because we have come
to understand how and
what we worship, that we
might come unto our Father
in the name of our Savior Jesus
Christ. We receive living water thru
our faithfulness, when we are washed
clean from the blood and sins
of this generation.

When we are baptized, the Spirit finds expression as a light within each of us. Even the worst among us may be recommended to our Heavenly Father if we have been washed in the cleansing waters.

We are baptized with the hope of "eternal life, which God, that cannot lie, promised before the world began." (Titus 1:2). When we fail to live up to the laws of the Gospel, The Plan of Mercy will intervene in our behalf, through repentance.

Each of us
begins a second-mile
journey as we step out of
the font following our baptism.
We burst free of the shackles that
had aforetime limited the expression
of our potential. We receive the Holy
Ghost, which is a gift of spiritual
independence that can disperse
the darkness as it removes
the veil of insensitivity
to our destiny.

We are baptized
by immersion in water,
that we might feel not only
the spiritual significance, but also
the physical intensity, of the promises
we make with our Heavenly Father. At our
baptism, we feel a palpable covenant of peace
that washes over us in concentric waves,
influencing everything in its path.

The
Lord Jesus Christ,
Who is both our Mentor
and our Exemplar, descended
beneath us all, both spiritually
and physically when He was
baptized in Jordan, which
is the lowest body of
fresh water upon
the face of the
earth.

Baptism at the age of eight captures the heart of children before they have been exposed to cankering influences and corrosive elements, and long before their hearts are fixed upon temporal things, their spirituality has been diminished, and the things of God are no longer part of their daily experience. Better than the rest of us, little children have a capacity to "lay aside the things of this world, and seek for the things of a better." (D&C 25:10).

When we ponder
our baptismal covenant, and
our responsibility to be ministers
of Christ, we will intuitively respond
to the invitation of President Gordon
B. Hinckley, to do a little better, to be a
little more kind, to be a little more merciful,
and a little more forgiving; "to put behind us our
weaknesses of the past, and go forth with new
energy and increased resolution to improve
the world about us, in our homes, in
our places of employment," and
"in our social activities."

Baptism attunes
us to the cries of the
downtrodden, and to the
needs of our fellow travelers,
and to be benevolently blind
to their shortcomings.

We are baptized
with an invitation to
write our own chapter of
The Greatest Story Ever Told.
Afterward, gone are the days when
we would have been content to
build upon the sepulchres
of the fathers.

"For the gate by which (we) should enter is repentance and baptism by water; and then cometh a remission of (our) sins by fire and by the Holy Ghost." This puts us on the "strait and narrow path that leads to eternal life." (2 Nephi 31:17-18).

"If it so be that ye believe in Christ, and are baptized, first with water, then with fire and with the Holy Ghost, following the example of our Savior, according to that which he hath commanded us, it shall be well with you in the day of judgment." (Mormon 7:10).

"The baptismal font was instituted as a similitude of the grave." (D&C 128:13).

"Adam
cried unto the Lord,
and he was caught away by
the Spirit of the Lord, and was
carried down into the water, and
was laid under the water, and was
brought forth out of the water. And
thus he was baptized, and the Spirit
of God descended upon him, and
thus he was born of the Spirit,
and became quickened
in the inner man."
(Moses 6:65-66).

We are baptized as a testament that "the works, and the designs, and the purposes of God cannot be frustrated, neither can they come to naught." (D&C 3:1). The Plan of Salvation is The Plan of Redemption, The Plan of Mercy, and especially it is God's Plan of Happiness, by making it possible for imperfect beings to be transformed by the covenant, and to rise in the resurrection, to live with Him eternally.

We are baptized that
we might lend our support
to the declaration made by the
Gods "that their plan was good."
(Abraham 4:21). When Jesus Christ
stepped forward to offer Himself as
the Lamb Who was slain from before
the foundation of the world, The Plan
shifted into a higher gear, by allowing
our Father's spirit children to come to
earth and die without repentance, but
at the same time, without jeopardizing
the continuity of their eternal destiny,
because of the vicarious work for the
dead to be performed in their behalf
by latter-day saviors on Mount Zion,
who faithfully attend the temples
of the Lord that are scattered
all across the earth in
the Last Days.

We are baptized in consequence of the "evils and designs which do and will exist in the hearts of conspiring men (and women) in the last days." (D&C 89:4). Angels will attend us after we have entered the Fold. They will go before our faces, and be on our right hand and on our left, and the Spirit of the Lord shall be in our heats, and heavenly angels will gather around us, to bear us up. (See D&C 84:88).

All of God's children are
invited to participate in the ordinance
of baptism. There are no height or weight
restrictions, no social, economic, cultural,
intellectual, or emotional prerequisites,
and no ecclesiastical qualifications,
other than to evince pure faith
that leads to repentance, with
a sincere desire to receive
forgiveness of
sin.

Alma taught that in the absence of repentance for their sins, and without their consecration thru baptism, Adam and Eve would have ultimately been miserable. To be certain, they would have lived forever, but it would have been in an unrelenting state of alienation from the presence of God.

God knows
what is best and
He has confidence
in our divine potential
to develop His nature. He
commands us to repent, to be
baptized, and to develop perfect
faith. Because these realistic goals
are easily within the reach of all
of His children, they become the
basic requirements for those
who hope to one day gain
readmittance to His
Kingdom.

The Devil's bribery stands in sharp contrast and in opposition to the blessings that follow our baptism.

Baptism
shepherds us past
the growing pains and
mental, emotional, physical,
and spiritual instability that are
related to early childhood
development.

Satan, who was a liar from the beginning, even now continues his efforts to foil The Plan of Salvation by the substitution of his own counterfeit, unworkable alternative that would not require repentance, baptism, or the Atonement. Fortunately, in the Council in Heaven, we were able to see through his deception. We still do.

Faith is dead, without the accompanying work of repentance that is made possible by the Atonement. Even great faith lacks the power to save us from the unalterable demands of Justice. So that Mercy might prevail, God provided us with baptism.

Standing in opposition to grace is a darkness that is so great that it has the potential to cover the earth, and gross darkness the people. Without repentance, baptism, and the Atonement, we would become subject to the evil source of that darkness, to rise no more.

It is for
our benefit
that we become
acquainted with evil
as well as with good, with
pain as well as with pleasure,
with darkness as well as with light,
with error as well as with truth, and
with punishment for the infraction of
God's eternal laws, as well as with the
blessings that follow our obedience. Our
baptism was designed to be an ace in
the hole, that through the Atonement
we could still conclude our mortal
mission and return to our Heavenly
Father in a state of holiness,
pure, and without
spot.

We are baptized "for the perfecting of the saints, for the work of the ministry, (and) for the edifying of the body of Christ." (Ephesians 4:12). The Saints are like snowflakes, that are one of nature's most fragile creations. Although delicate in structure, just look at what snowflakes, and members of the Church, can do when they stick together.

We are baptized
that those who have
died without having had
the opportunity to hear about
The Plan of Salvation might also
partake of eternal life. The Atonement
sets the standard of vicarious work for the
dead. In our day, the Savior has delegated
authority to the members of His Church to
follow His example, to act in behalf of
those who are unable to perform the
saving ordinances for themselves,
since they have passed beyond
the veil and are living in
the Spirit World while
they patiently await
the resurrection.

We are baptized
that, with the gentle
instruction of the Spirit,
we might become better at
forging relationships on
earth that will endure
in heaven.

When we walk
in the footsteps
of Jesus Christ with real
intent, by repenting of our
sins, we witness unto the Father
that we are willing to take upon
ourselves the name of Christ, by
baptism - yea, by following
our Lord and our Savior
down into the water.
(See 2 Nephi 31:13).

"My people have gone astray from my precepts, and have not kept mine ordinances, which I gave unto their fathers. And they have not observed mine anointing, and the burial, or baptism wherewith I commanded them."
(J.S.T. Genesis 17:5).

"Know ye not that, so many of us as were baptized into Jesus Christ were baptized into his death? Therefore, we are buried with him by baptism into death, that like as Christ was raised up from the dead by the glory of the Father, even so we also should walk in newness of life" through the symbolism of being born again, with baptism by immersion. (Romans 6:3).

"Be humble, and be submissive and gentle; easy to be entreated; full of patience and long-suffering; being temperate in all things; being diligent in keeping the commandments of God at all times; asking for whatsoever things ye stand in need, both spiritual and temporal, always returning thanks unto God for whatsoever things ye do receive. And see that ye have faith, hope, and charity, and then will ye always abound in good works."
(Alma 7:23-24).

"The harder the conflict, the more glorious the triumph. What we obtain too cheap, we esteem too lightly; 'tis dearness only that gives everything its value. Heaven knows how to put a proper price upon its goods." (Tom Paine, "Common Sense"). It would be strange, indeed, if such a celestial article as baptism should not be highly rated.

Immersion in water
is symbolic of the burial of
Christ. (See 3 Nephi 11:23). Joseph
Smith said the repentant are "baptized
after the manner of his burial, being buried in
the water in his name, and this according to the
commandment which he has given — That
by keeping the commandments they
might be washed and cleansed
from all their sins."
(D&C 76:51-52).

We have no
proof until we act upon
the basis of belief. Then comes the
ratification of the reality, manifest as a
spiritual confirmation, but only after we
act in faith. That is the essence of
why James taught that "faith,
if it hath not works, is
dead, being alone."
(James 2:17).

After our baptism,
we press forward, not
with the crowd who jostles
for position in the circus of
telestial trivialities, but rather
with the Saints who seek wisdom
and the mysteries of God.
We get our fix when we
focus our attention
on the stars.

When we
are baptized, we
adopt a culture of
faith that embraces us
to help insulate us from
worldly influences. It alerts
us to Satan's misdirection, that
attempts to lead us from brilliant,
dazzling white, through every shade
of grey, to that fathomless black which,
by subtraction, is the absence of every
uplifting thought, word, deed, or
sustaining principle.

Baptism is the
catalyst that propels us upward
toward a discovery of the personal
levels of experience with the Savior, for
when He speaks of "knowing Him," He must be
referring to a special sense of the word. It is not
enough that we know about Him by reading the
Gospels, or by listening to others speak of
Him. We must know Him through the
bonds of common experience
and common feeling.

Baptism
can give us
the perspective
to see adversity
as a diamond dust
that polishes us to a
high luster, instead of
an abrasive that wears
us down and grinds
us up.

We are baptized
in white clothing that
is a gentle reminder of
the purity of the ordinance
and the proximity of the
Spirit.

Baptism fans
the fire of our
resolve with faith.
We hope and pray to
have courage to change
the things we can, for the
serenity to accept the things
we cannot, and for the
wisdom to know the
difference.

Our baptism
endows us with
the strength to watch
ourselves judiciously, to
be the meticulous guardians
of our thoughts, the scrupulous
custodians of our words, and the
prudent caretakers of our deeds, to
fastidiously observe the commandments
of God, and to continue evenly in the faith.

Our temporal
baggage can create imbalance
that leads to confusion. Baptism jars
us out of our collective complacency by
upsetting the stagnation of the status
quo. It invites us to enjoy a settled
conviction in our minds by getting
our juices flowing, prodding
us to constructively expend
our energy, and putting
our agency to work.

All
who enter the
waters of baptism
have a divine destiny
and are the nobility of
heaven. They are counted
among those of a choice
and chosen generation.
(See 1 Peter 2:9).

For this
end was the
law given, that
we might be made
alive in Christ, and
this because of our
faith in baptism as
an ordinance of
the Gospel.

We live in the world
but we make sure that our
feet are firmly planted on Gospel
sod so that we can recognize sounding
brass and tinkling cymbals for what they
really are. Baptism catalyzes a mystical and
metaphysical transformation wherein we have
been figuratively born of God. With new
eyes, we can see from here to eternity,
and with new ears, we can hear the
word of the Lord above so many
competing voices.

Simply put, baptism
exposes us to the process by
which we progress. Heavenly Father
designed baptism so that He could test
our mettle. This is why the courage to be
true to our convictions is so intimately tied
to righteousness. Only when we act on the basis
of faith will we receive a confirmation of the
power behind the ordinance of baptism,
as feelings of self-confidence grow
and purposeful action replaces
our tentative overtures.

With our baptism
the Light of our lives
grows brighter and even
"brighter until the perfect
day." (D&C 50:24). "Trailing
clouds of glory do we come,
from God, who is our Home."
(William Wordsworth).

When we come
up out of the baptismal font,
we are easily entreated, and we
are firm in our obedience to every
one of the commandments of God. For
the conflagration of sin to be initiated,
all that is needed is combustible fuel, an
ignition temperature, and oxygen. We must
live in the world, but we don't have to be
of the world. We can't allow the heat of
the moment to get the better of us. Our
baptism introduces us to the strait
and narrow way that avoids the
Devil's ammunition dumps, as
well as an open flame.
After our baptism, we
learn not to play
with matches.

Baptism is universally applicable. It allows each of us to break free from our limiting beliefs, those stories we tell ourselves that sabotage our best efforts. Baptism, on the other hand, unleashes the awesome power of our potential. Its magic is waiting for our wits to grow sharper, so that we can be inspired by the Holy Ghost.

We are baptized
in a palpable expression
of the Doctrine of Christ. In
The Book of Mormon, Nephi clearly
explained this doctrine; it is that all who
have faith in Jesus Christ and truly repent of
their sins, entering into a baptismal covenant with
Him, will receive the Holy Ghost, Who will then
direct their way, showing them the things they
must do to merit the grace of God and
inherit salvation.

The Last Days mirror those of Mormon, who wrote that "there were sorceries, and witchcrafts, and magics, and the power of the evil one was wrought upon all the face of the land" because of the lack of faith of the people. (Mormon 1:19). Baptism is the spiritual equivalent of enjoying a power bar or energy drink 30 minutes before engaging in physical activity.

"In moments of deep reflection, as at the waters of baptism, we envision "stepping on shore, and finding it heaven! We visualize taking hold of a hand, and finding it God's hand. We dream of passing from storm and tempest to an unbroken calm, and of waking up, and finding it home." (Anonymous).

With baptism, we
receive a variety of spiritual
gifts that can be the antidote for
the poisonous telestial tendencies
that suppress the expression
of celestial sureties.

By coherently
stitching together
the foundation principles
of faith and repentance into
an understandable pattern, baptism
makes it possible for the power of the
word and the witness of truth to be
discovered without the need for
external warrant.

When we are baptized, the cobwebs are swept from our minds and we are blessed with the visitation of the Holy Ghost, which does nothing short of filling us with hope and perfect love.

Baptism
is the token
of our acceptance
of our Father's invitation
to join Him in His work and
glory, which is to bring to pass
our immortality and eternal life.
Some may consider the commitment
too costly, but countless witnesses
have testified how obedience has
become, for them, the perfect
law of liberty.

The
steadiness
of baptism stands
as the polar opposite of
the intellectual instability
and spiritual schizophrenia
that we witness all about
us in the world today.

Baptism opens
a portal to principles,
ordinances, and covenants that
enable us to be sanctified, to be worthy
to live again in a state of holiness in the
presence of our Heavenly Father. Because
of baptism, we may all "continue in the
supplicating of his grace," to one day
stand blameless before Him
at His Pleasing Bar.
(Alma 7:3).

Our covenants, beginning with baptism, reposition the riches of eternity so that they are within our grasp. They expand our vision beyond physical laws that pertain only to the temporal world, toward an appreciation of Gospel principles that relate to time as well as to the eternities. Baptism invites us to reach out and touch the face of God.

Baptism empowers us to follow through; to be successful. The Church is the vehicle that makes this possible and the priesthood is the fuel that drives the engine of our faith.

Baptism
encourages
us to give ourselves
completely and without
reservation, that we might
enjoy a state of harmony with
God and synchronization with the
eternities. It beckons us to search
without ceasing, that we might
discover within His nature
the divine center of
our faith.

Values are beliefs that may change with circumstances because they are culturally or personally determined. Baptism is the tangible expression of a Gospel principle, a truth that is eternally valid. Its correct understanding is essential, because as a foundation ordinance it lies at the very heart of the doctrine of the Gospel of Jesus Christ.

With baptism,
Mercy satisfies Justice,
and the penitent faithful
receive a remission of sins
in a symbolic rite of
purification.

When the law is woven
into the sinews of our souls, that
it becomes the tapestry of our lives and
is the very pattern upon which we trace our
progress along the path of progression, our
"minds become single to God, and the
days will come that (we) shall
see him; for he will unveil
his face" unto us.
(D&C 88:68).

Our
baptism carries us, as on
the wings of angels, far from
the madding crowd, to caress the
tender chords of human associations,
of gratitude, loyalty, and appreciation, of
selflessness, helpfulness and forgiveness, of
friendship, love, and compassion. It moves
us with truth discovered and accepted,
of beauty created and enjoyed, of
goodness deepened and made
manifest in life.

We are baptized as a witness that "the Lord God will do nothing" in the Last Days "but he revealeth his secret unto his servants the prophets." (Amos 3:7).

For
The Plan
to succeed,
there needs to
be opposition, light
and darkness, pleasure
and pain, good and evil,
and happiness and misery,
which makes baptism essential,
because, let's face it, most of us
lack the spiritual horsepower to
consistently choose the right,
much less to save ourselves.
Virtually all of us need
God every hour of
our lives.

We are baptized
with the realization
that when the Lord gives
us commandments, He also
prepares ways for us to accomplish
the tasks that are set before us. We see
what might be best for ourselves and for
the Kingdom of God, develop a testimony
that it should be, and then work with all our
capacity to make it happen, whatever the cost
might be. Then, when we are so richly blessed
far beyond the measure that we deserve, the
price, once paid so painfully, is recalled in
gladness. We receive full value.

Following the baptism of Joseph Smith and Oliver Cowdery, they wrote: "Our minds being now enlightened, we began to have the scriptures laid open to our understandings, and the true meaning and intention of their more mysterious passages revealed unto us in a manner which we never could attain to previously, nor ever before had thought of." (J.S.H. 1:74).

There is priesthood power in the words of the ordinance of baptism to "break mountains, to divide the seas, to dry up waters, to turn them out of their course; to put at defiance the armies of nations, to divide the earth, to break every band, to stand in the presence of God." (J.S.T. Genesis 14:30-31).

After the Fall,
the portal to Eden
may have swung shut,
but as it did so, another
door opened that introduced
Adam and Eve to a secret garden
accessible only to those who would
utilize the power of the Atonement.
By obedience to the ordinance of
baptism, they would be able to
experience both good and evil,
pleasure and pain, as well as
light and darkness, in the
white hot crucible
of experience.

We are baptized
that we might rejoice
in our characterization by
others as peculiar people, for
we have become eyewitnesses
to the vitalization of The
Plan of our Creator.

Those
who zip along
in the fast lane of
life can far too easily
blow right past the celestial
signpost of baptism, that would
have alerted them to move over
into the exit lane that leads
to the gates of heaven.

Perfect faith impels us to action. When we follow up on our righteous impressions, it is as though we have enjoyed God's perfect understanding. We willingly submit to baptism.

Without
our baptism that
follows on the heels
of repentance, we cannot
reasonably expect to inherit
the glory of celestial realms;
especially if we have aforetime
been agreeable to abide by only
telestial or terrestrial principles
that put fewer demands upon
our discipleship.

When
we exercise
our free will that is
always carried out in
an atmosphere of opposition,
undesirable consequences are
likely to follow. These effects
can only be mitigated by
repentance and by
baptism.

We are born again through our baptism. When we have been washed clean from the blood and sins of the world, we are oriented more to the expansive laws of the eternities than we are to the restrictive postulates of our physical surroundings. This is why our spirits must be nurtured by repentance before we can become candidates for baptism.

We know by
the casualty count from
the ideological war that was
fought in heaven, that there were
some of our brothers and sisters who
forfeit their privilege to obtain a body.
For those who remained faithful came
humbling liabilities, for The Plan of
Salvation required that the Creator
die for our sins, conditional
only upon repentance
unto baptism.

Baptism will always be waiting in the wings, to be applied as a balm to repair bruised egos, bitter feelings, and battered birthrights.

It is
our honesty with
ourselves that tests the
mettle of our convictions.
With our commitment to be
baptized, we are putting our
money where our mouth is. We
have no proof until we act on
the basis of trust. Then, comes
the confirmation of the reality
as feelings of self-confidence
grow and purposeful actions
replace tentative overtures.
In effect, we let go
and let God.

After we
have submitted
to baptism, the Spirit
will teach us how to become
engaged in fashioning defensive
weapons in the armory of thought.
It is with these tools that the Lord
will show us just how we will be
able to construct the heavenly
fortifications of love, joy,
strength, and peace.

When we are baptized,
Jesus Christ, or his earthly
representative, invites us by
name to become His disciples.
The ordinance confirms that all
three members of the Godhead
are willing to pause in Their
busy schedules to witness
our baptism, as well as
to welcome us into
the fold.

"The Lamb of God ... fulfil(ed) all righteousness in being baptized by water." (2 Nephi 31:6).

"Heaven
lies about us
in our infancy. Shades
of the prison house begin
to close upon the growing boy.
But he beholds the light and whence
it flows; he sees it in his joy. The youth,
who daily farther from the east must travel,
still is nature's priest. And by the vision splendid,
is on his way attended. At length, the man
perceives it die away, and fade into
the light of common day."
(Wordsworth).

Baptism is of
such power that it drives the
law into our inward parts, so that
it is written upon our hearts. A mighty
change takes place as we experience the
process of sanctification. When we are
born again, the desired result of all
Gospel-oriented teaching has been
achieved, and we have no more
disposition to do evil, but to
do good continually.
(See Mosiah 5:2).

In perfect harmony, the Godhead promotes the doctrine of Christ with one shared goal: To bring us to the waters of baptism, and thereafter to the portal of the Celestial Kingdom.

Angels will attend us after we have entered the fold. "For I will go before your face," promised the Lord. "I will be on your right hand, and on your left, and my Spirit shall be in your hearts, and mine angels round about you, to bear you up." (D&C 84:88).

Baptism is the evidence that
we have exercised our faith. As we
gain spiritual maturity, our faith becomes
perfect knowledge. Initially, faith is to believe
what we do not see, and the reward of faith is
to see what we believe. The process by which
faith is developed is one of testing. The
Lord gives certain principles, and by
obedience to them, blessings
and power follow.

We are
baptized
to stand tall
for those who
may lack the
power to do
so on their
own.

We
will always
be subject to the
effects of adversity and
opposition, but without the
therapeutic benefits of baptism,
we may needlessly suffer from a stiff
neck that prevents us from looking up to
Heavenly Father for guidance, over to
priesthood leaders for counsel,
around to seek out those in
need, and down in an
attitude of humility.

Baptism
helps us to get
off religious roundabouts.
We "come unto Christ, and (are)
perfected in him, and deny (ourselves)
of all ungodliness; and if (we) shall deny
(our)selves of all ungodliness, and love God
with all (our) might, mind and strength,
then is his grace sufficient for (us),
that by his grace (we) may
be perfect in Christ."
(Moroni 10:32).

"There is no regularly constituted church on earth, nor any person authorized to administer any church ordinance (such as baptism); nor can there be until new apostles are sent by the Great Head of the Church, for Whose Coming I am seeking." (Roger Williams).

"I will give unto the children of men line upon line, precept upon precept, here a little and there a little; and blessed are those who hearken unto my precepts, and lend an ear unto my counsel, for they shall learn wisdom; for unto him that receiveth, I will give more."
(2 Nephi 28:30).

Baptism is
a principle that
can only be tested when
we nurture a companionship
with the Spirit, for when we
fall under its spell, we
are at-one with the
Savior of the
world.

We are baptized
in an affirmation of
our support of family
values. Baptism directs our
efforts toward relationships
that are the basic building
blocks of eternity.

One of the purposes of our baptism is that it catalyzes our resolve to bear our testimony to the world of the things we have learned by the power of the Spirit, so that their experience can be as profound as it was for those on the Day of Pentecost, when the witness of Peter and the other apostles carried the day as it penetrated the hearts of all who listened, and instilled within them the desire to inquire: "What must we do if we want to inherit eternal life?"

Baptism blesses us with the privilege to "mourn with those that mourn." (Mosiah 18:9). We smile with all our heart and with all our might. If we are nothing else, we can be the smile on the faces of those who mourn, or stand in need of comfort.

We
are baptized
to capture "the peace
of God, which passeth all
understanding." (Philippians 4:7).
Baptism gives us the opportunity
to have the best of both worlds;
to live on the earth, but still
enjoy a quiet refuge from
telestial turmoil.

Repentance
is nurtured within
the rich culture medium
of faith, validated by baptism
in a metaphysical reunion with
God. It is witnessed in the fiery
cauldron of the Spirit, in the
only way that is possible,
to ransom us from
our sins.

It makes
very little difference
to our Father in Heaven
whether we are combating the
influences of the Seven Deadly
Sins, or the garden-variety of
transgressions that we commit
every day; the doctrine of the
Atonement stipulates that we
go through the process of
repentance before we
submit to baptism
by immersion.

Baptism stares into the jaws of spiritual death without averting its eyes. It was not the Savior, but the deceiver who was the first to blink before he was unceremoniously cast out of heaven, a fallen son of the morning!

From a position of power, the Savior has negotiated with Justice to purchase our sins with the legally recognized currency of the Atonement. His voluntary act of sacrifice is perfectly balanced and attuned to accomplish the task at hand, to overcome death and hell, only subject to our willingness to submit to baptism by immersion for the remission of sins.

Baptism
provides a way
for us to increase our
metaphysical metabolism,
to burn away as much of the
fat of faithlessness as we can
when our hearts are broken
in the fiery hot crucible
of contrition.

Our
exercise
of free will in
an atmosphere of
opposition propels us
onward toward immortality
and eternal life, as long as we
rely on the ordinance of baptism
and the Atonement of Christ
to keep the sand of sin
out of our gears.

The Day
of Judgment
does not lie over a
distant horizon, but is
today. We speak, think, and
act according to the celestial,
terrestrial, and telestial laws that
are before us. Just as a barometer
is used to measure the direction in
which the weather is headed, our
desire to honor our baptismal
covenant helps us to be aware
of the direction we must
follow if we hope to
regain the shelter
of our heavenly
home.

Those who truly appreciate the power of the ordinance of baptism are able to visualize the Celestial Kingdom. They use the Atonement of Christ to move in its direction. They follow the admonition of the Savior: "Seek ye first the kingdom of God, and his righteousness; and all these things shall be added unto you." (Matthew 6:33).

Baptism helps us
to chart the unknown
possibilities of existence.
We sweep aside the self-limiting
belief that "the sky is the limit." In
its stead, we substitute the mind
and soul expanding certainty
that "the wide expanse of
heaven is the limit."

We are baptized
that we might join
the ranks of member
missionaries. Curiously,
it is through His disciples,
that the Lord shows the
children of men that
He is able to do His
own work.

The
world attempts
to make changes
from the outside, and
fails miserably. But baptism
changes us from the inside, and
succeeds brilliantly. We are thus
created to reach our potential
in both the image and
likeness of God,
our Father.

Baptism is the
great equalizer
for Heavenly Father's
children. The ordinances
that are part of The Plan will
always stand ready to save our
souls, but in the meantime, we
may worship Almighty God
according to the dictates
of our conscience.

After our baptism, the Holy Ghost guides us to covenants relating to the priesthood and the temple. "I will give unto the children of men line upon line, precept upon precept, here a little and there a little; and blessed are those who hearken unto my precepts, and lend an ear unto my counsel, for they shall learn wisdom; for unto him that receiveth I will give more." (2 Nephi 28:30).

We are baptized
that we might pause,
and ponder the things
that are really important
in our lives. Reflection is
a good thing, especially
when it is the light of
Christ that shines on
our countenances.

Submitting to the ordinance of baptism provides the mortar that holds together the building blocks of character. It is the consummate compilation of affirmative action.

Those who refuse the Spirit's invitation to be baptized have hard hearts, stiff-necks, and are overtly and covertly rebellious. They lack the malleability and the pliability of those who are humbly repentant.

Only with
our baptism does
mortality become the
wonderful center for the
talented and gifted that
it was envisioned to
be by the Merciful
Plan of our
Father.

Sometimes,
it is only after
we have enrolled
in the graduate school
of hard knocks, and have
pre-paid the required tuition,
that we obtain the credits that
are earned by obedience to the
curriculum, and learn how to
be charitable to our brothers
and sisters. We recall the
charge that was given by
Alma so long ago, as
he stood beside the
still waters of
Mormon.

Blind opposition, enmity, hatred, hostility, inflexibility, and intolerance are the raw manifestations of pride, but these are overwhelmed by the accommodation, charity, faith, approachability, hope, and sociability of the those who come to the waters of baptism.

As the battle rages in the hearts of men, those who have been baptized live their lives in crescendo. The deafening roar of their righteousness commands the attention of the angels in heaven who wield the sword of Justice, and who only await upon God's command before letting it fall upon an unrepentant world.

We are baptized that we might find happiness, peace, and rest; that we might obtain the blessings of the fathers. These include the fruits of faith whose source is the Atonement of Jesus Christ.

The worth of principles is validated through personal witness, or testimony. Our desire to be baptized becomes the outward expression of our personal dedication to obedience. It is the public manifestation of our desire to have a private covenant relationship with God. It is our voluntary surrender of agency to a higher power, and the subjugation of our won't, to His will.

We are baptized
that we might have
opportunities to bear
each other's burdens. It
does not debate the merits
of the petitions of the weak
and impoverished who need
our aid and it turns a blind
eye to the prejudices that
threaten to influence the
depth and breadth of
our compassion.

Baptism is special,
because there are rhythms
in nature that we feel only
when we are in harmony
with eternal principles.

We are baptized
in order to be perfected
in our Savior, Jesus Christ. Our
spiritual awakening progresses for
as long as we are learning. We take
solace in the scriptures, where, although
we are admonished 154 times to be perfect,
we are also encouraged 129 times to
"learn" and 995 times to "begin."

Baptism is a great place to learn the grammar of the Gospel. It is the exclamation point of our repentance process. We approach the ordinance with confidence that "at the banquet of consequences, we will be able to bow our heads in reverence, rather than hang them in shame, in the presence of God, Who will be there." (Marion D. Hanks).

We are baptized that we might be "slow to be led to do iniquity; and quick to hearken unto the words of the Lord." (Helaman 7:7). There needs to be opposition in all things, and the righteous are always at the risk of yielding to the temptation to partake of corrosive cocktails of convenience that are forever being offered by a beguiling bartender named Beelzebub.

It is at
our baptisms that we feel
the gentle caress of the hands
of the Master Potter, as He turns our
lives with the hand of time. We give Him
permission, as the Artisan of our destiny, to
mold us and shape us. (See Jeremiah 18:6). We
are the clay, and He is our potter; and we are the
work of His hands. (See Isaiah 64:8). As our
thoughts turn to the Savior, we remain
impressionable and pliable to
the things of the Spirit.

It is after our baptism that
we are immersed within a heaven
sent curriculum, where we learn to
speak the language of the Spirit. We
receive the celestial antidotes for
poisonous telestial tendencies
that threaten to choke out
the expression of God's
word and will.

Baptism encourages us
to step back, inhale deeply,
take a moment, and focus on the
things of importance in our busy lives.
The covenant gently guides us into
the warm embrace of daily
spiritual experiences.

The voice of warning is that all men and women everywhere, and boys and girls also, must repent and be baptized. Those who reject the glad message, the rebellious in heart and the enthusiastically ignorant, will be pierced with sorrow when they finally recognize their folly.

Our baptism will
leave the world a better place
than when we found it. When we pass
beyond the veil, we will leave our loved
ones with a legacy of both intangible and
tangible remembrances. We will leave them
with our testimony. We will leave them with
gratitude for the privilege and blessing to
have been knit together in families that
are the corporeal building blocks of
our Heavenly Father's great
Plan of Happiness.

It was an essential element of The Plan of Salvation, ordained in the grand Council in Heaven before the world was, that little children who died before the age of accountability would be saved in the Celestial Kingdom by the power of the Atonement. "If not so, God is a partial God, and also a changeable God, and a respecter of persons; for how many little children have died without baptism!" (Moroni 8:12).

"Wherefore, my beloved brethren, can we follow Jesus, save we shall be willing to keep the commandments of the Father? And the Father said: Repent ye, repent ye, and be baptized in the name of my Beloved Son." (2 Nephi 31:10-11).

"Ye must repent, and be baptized in my name, and become as a little child, or ye can in nowise inherit the kingdom of God." (3 Nephi 11:38).

We are the "elect according to the foreknowledge of God the Father, through sanctification of the Spirit, unto obedience and sprinkling of the blood of Jesus Christ." (1 Peter 1:2).

Our baptism protects us from spiritual identity theft. Of the truth that we have a Father in Heaven, there is no question, for "the Spirit itself beareth witness with our spirit, that we are the children of God." (Romans 8:16). We know this intuitively. How sweet it is to hear Primary age children as young as three sing the songs of Zion that declare we are the children of God.

When we are
baptized, we experience the
spiritual equivalent of unwrapping
a Wonka Bar that contains one of only
five Golden Tickets. But we do so without
the rush of the sensory over-stimulation that
has become so prevalent in our self-indulgent
society. In its place, as a fire in the sky, the
atmosphere in the theater of life is charged
with an electricity that is evidence of the
merger of the universal encouragement
of the Light of Christ with the pointed
and providential guidance that is
provided by the Holy Ghost.

While baptism nurtures the
development of personality
traits that are in concordance
with the symmetry of heaven, sin
is harmful because it destroys our
ability to nurture the equilibrium
that is a defining characteristic
of those who inherit eternal
life. In God's nature, there
is neither variableness,
nor shadow of
turning.

Every baptism
is a little packet of
light that contributes
just the right amount
of illumination to a
dark world.

We are baptized
so that we might unite
ourselves with the mechanism
by which eternal principles are
communicated. The ordinance is
a manifestation of the practical
application of the power of the
Holy Ghost to be a Revelator
and a Testator.

To whom but God can we turn for the assurance that liberates us from fear, doubt, the apprehension of danger, the turmoil of the world, and from the vagaries of men? Only when we have cast off the self-limiting conditions and self-defeating behaviors that blind us to a larger view of life, will we enjoy a settled conviction of the truth in our minds.

"Little children need no repentance, neither baptism. Behold, baptism is unto repentance to the fulfilling the commandments unto the remission of sins. But little children are alive in Christ, even from the foundation of the world."
(Moroni 8:11-12).

Baptism open
up windows of opportunity
to better understand the principles
of the Gospel, that are mysteries to those
who have not spiritually prepared themselves for
personal revelation from God. The Lord has
assured us that we "shall know of a
surety that these things are true,
for from heaven will (He)
declare it unto (us)."
(D&C 5:12).

Our
baptism
launches
a covenant
relationship
with the Lord
that invites us
to stand with Him,
and to weigh in on
His side of the scale,
even as the counterfeit
coins of Satan's spurious
currency clatter down on
the other side of the scale
in a cacophony of
confusion.

"For by the water (we) keep the commandment; by the Spirit (we) are justified, and by the blood (we) are sanctified." (Moses 6:60).

With our
baptism comes
"the remission of sins
(which) bringeth meekness,
and lowliness of heart; and
because of meekness and lowliness
of heart cometh the visitation of the
Holy Ghost, which Comforter filleth with
hope and perfect love, which love endureth
by diligence unto prayer, until the end
shall come, when all the saints
shall dwell with God."
(Moroni 8:26).

"Know ye not that, so many of us as were baptized into Jesus Christ were baptized into his death? Therefore, we are buried with him by baptism into death, that like as Christ was raised up from the dead by the glory of the Father, even so we also should walk in newness of life" through the symbolism of being born again, with baptism by immersion. (Romans 6:3).

Sometimes,
when we brush against
the veil, we feel inner stirrings
that are the harmonic vibrations of the
music of a heavenly choir, and we hear the
indistinct murmurings of the voices of angelic
messengers. This is one of the reasons that we
are baptized; that while we yet dwell on
the earth, we might nevertheless be
blessed to be "partakers of
the divine nature."
(2 Peter 1:4).

The powers of
heaven and earth amplify
each other, and carry us along
on waves of the Spirit. With baptism, all
our trappings and pretenses are shorn away,
outward observance and phylacteries
are stripped from the ritual of
our worship, and only our
true feelings remain.

There will
be a day for
the faithful, as
at their baptism,
when the sun shall
not go down, "neither
shall the moon withdraw
itself. For the Lord shall
be their everlasting light."
(Isaiah 60:20).

Through
the workings of
the Spirit and by the
power of our faith, when
we are baptized, we see all the
way to heaven, with the capacity
to be carried beyond the perceptible
and palpable confines of this world
to a place where boundaries are
blurred, and the barricade of
borders evaporates in a
flood of light.

Baptism directs us to "press forward" with complete dedication and with "steadfastness," or with confidence and a firm determination in Christ, "having a perfect brightness of hope," or perfect faith, and charity, or "a love of God and of all men." If we do this, "feasting upon the word of Christ," by receiving strength and nourishment from the scriptures, and if we endure to the end, not in wickedness, but in righteousness, we "shall have eternal life," which is the greatest gift that God can bestow. (2 Nephi 31:20).

We are baptized
because of our testimony
that the principles governing
the Fall of Adam, as well as the
Savior's Atonement, were "great and
eternal purposes (that) were prepared
from the foundation of the world."
(Alma 42:26). Our baptism itself
testifies that we were willing
then, and are willing now,
to participate in
The Plan.

We are baptized
that we might honor
God and feel His love,
as we confess His hand in
all things, and strive to obey
all of His commandments. Jesus
Christ is our cornerstone; He is the
Architect of the cosmos, including the
"Pillars of Creation," elephant trunks
of interstellar gas and dust in the
Eagle Nebula, 7,000 light years
from earth.

At our baptism, we experience the excitement of being spiritually begotten of Him, and of having our hearts changed through faith on His name. We turn our thoughts to Him and feel His energy building within us.

"For behold, it is as easy to give heed to the word of Christ, which will point to you a straight course to eternal bliss, as it was for our fathers to give heed to this compass, which would point unto them a straight course to the promised land." (Alma 37: 44). As it was for Alma and his people, so it is for us. Christ is our Navigator. If we follow Him to the waters of baptism, we will find that no wind can blow except it fills our sails.

Because of our obedience that leads us to the waters of baptism, our foundation in the Kingdom of God is planted on bedrock, as was the wall that was built by an Irishman around his farm. When asked why he had built it five feet high and eight feet thick, he explained that if the wind ever blew so hard that it would topple over, his wall of protection would still be five feet thick. Baptism is such an ordinance. When we embrace it and are sheltered by the shield of faith, we will be able to withstand any wind that might blow.

Those who refuse to respond to the invitation of the missionaries to be baptized have more won't power than will power.

God encourages faithfulness, with an emphasis on the "ful." In its abundance, we find that we have more than enough, even a surplus, a surfeit, that is overflowing and brimming with possibilities, and when our cup runneth over, we will reflect that it was our submission to baptism that propelled us right into the embrace of eternity.

After we are baptized, our Heavenly Father often uses the Spirit to show us our weaknesses, for they can become a primer on midwifery, germinating the arduous process of the growth and development of our testimonies.

We must be baptized for the remission of sins. The foundation principle upon which the ordinance is anchored is based upon an injunction found throughout the canon of scripture: "Repent, and be baptized every one of you in the name of Jesus Christ for the remission of sins." (Acts 2:38).

There are no shades of grey
after we have received the ordinance of
baptism and our minds become "single to
God." (D&C 88:68). If we try to have it
both ways, our double mindedness will
create intellectual instability and
spiritual schizophrenia, for we
cannot be servants of the
Devil while purporting
to follow Christ.

The
process of
igniting our
dormant spirit,
or of kindling our
divine spark, or of
awakening our divine
potential to nurture the
God in embryo that is
within each of us, even
the acorn of a might
oak, is one of
being born
again.

Bathed in
the stunning clarity of
light, those who have been
baptized often stare in wide-
eyed wonder at the beautiful
simplicity of the interwoven
threads within the pattern of
Gospel principles that make
up the tapestry of The
Plan of Salvation.

The
indescribable peace
that follows our obedience
to the laws of repentance and
baptism repositions us so that a
greater reality falls within our
grasp. When we realize that we
are not alone, we will have
begun a journey that will
cover us in the stardust
of heaven, as we
mingle among
the Gods.

"Whoso believeth in me, and is baptized ... shall inherit the kingdom of God." (3 Nephi 11:33).

Our baptism is a reminder that the poor, the unlearned, the common person, and the native born, may equally come unto Christ. The beauty of the Gospel is that one size fits all. It is designed to meet the needs of all of the children of our Heavenly Father, from the greatest to the least of our brothers and sisters.

We cannot superficially whitewash our sins to cover them up, no matter how hard we try.

No matter how wide the net
is cast, science cannot explain
the flickering shadows of eternity
that dance around us at baptismal
services, as the features of heaven
are illuminated by the brightly
burning light of faith.

Baptism brings us into harmony with the eternities. It helps us to overcome the world with a freedom from confinement to the inexorable immutability of the destructive laws that govern our temporal world.

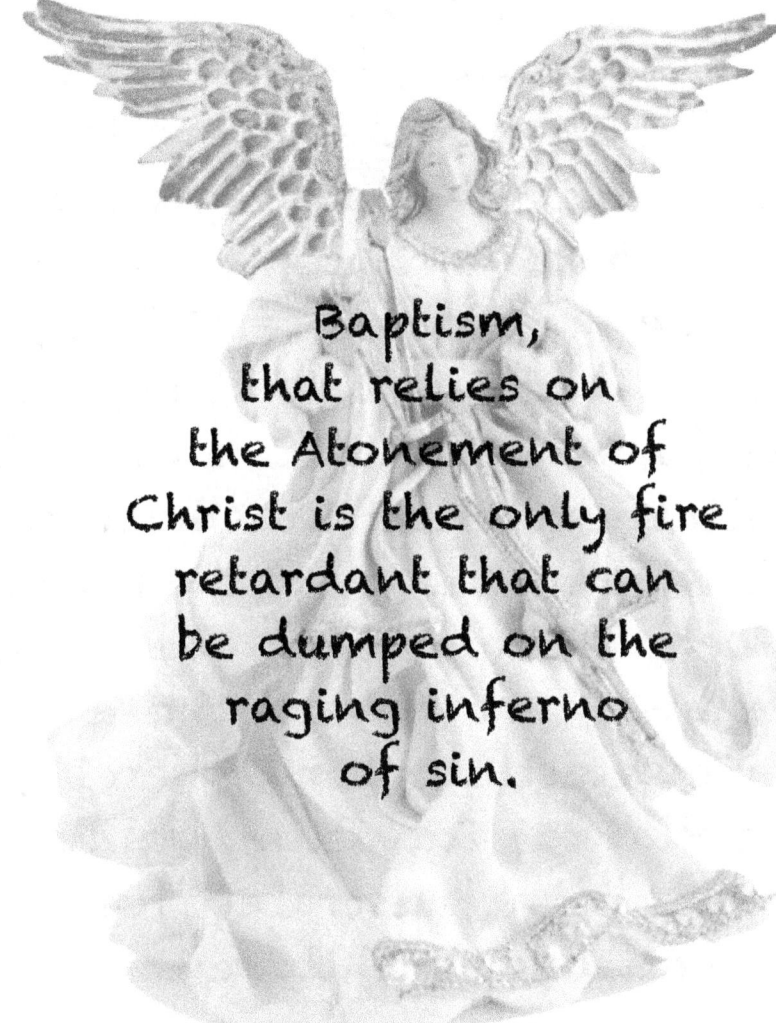

Baptism, that relies on the Atonement of Christ is the only fire retardant that can be dumped on the raging inferno of sin.

Without repentance leading to baptism, if they were to have partaken of the fruit of the Tree of Life, which is eternal life, or the highest expression of the love of God, it would not have been possible for Adam and Eve to sustain a celestial existence, inasmuch as in their current condition they would have been incapable of obedience to the laws that govern those who merit celestial glory. Thereby, the Plan of Salvation would have been frustrated for all of the children of God.

Once we
have committed ourselves
to baptism, our comprehension
of the covenant will flow easily and
poetically to our minds. Our persistence
and participation will lead to a practiced
fluency in the language of the Spirit that will
be the inevitable result of the inspiration that
must come to us as we approach our baptism
with faith, fasting, and prayer. As our minds
are enlightened, we will be launched into
a flowing stream of revelation as we
are carried in quickening currents
of direct experience with the
mind and will of God.

Against seemingly insurmountable odds, and in the face of an almost overwhelming darkness, those who have made the remarkable commitment to be baptized have somehow been able to break free of "the influence of that spirit which hath so strongly riveted the creeds of the fathers, who have inherited lies, upon the hearts of the children, and filled the world with confusion." (D&C 123:7).

We are baptized
that we might overcome
spiritual death, and come
into the presence of the Father,
the Son, and the Holy Ghost, Who
dazzle us with an endless reserve of
revelation that provides illumination to
every corner of our minds and our spirits.
The promises proffered by the combined
capacity of the intrinsic light possessed
by the Holy Trinity, then, is simply
beyond our comprehension.

Moroni
spoke plainly
and without ambiguity
about the first principles and
ordinances of the Gospel. "The
first fruits of repentance is baptism;
and baptism cometh by faith unto the
fulfilling the commandments; and the
fulfilling the commandments bringeth
remission of sins; and the remission of
sins bringeth meekness, and lowliness
of heart; and because of meekness
and lowliness of heart cometh the
visitation of the Holy Ghost."
(Moroni 8:25-26).

"This thing shall ye teach – repentance and baptism unto those who are accountable and capable of committing sin; yea, teach parents that they must repent and be baptized, and humble themselves as their little children, and they shall all be saved with their little children." (Moroni 8:10).

Our life-long
learning laboratory has given
each of us an opportunity to mold
our nature to more closely resemble
that of our Father in Heaven. He
initiated baptism to make
that metamorphosis
possible.

At our baptism, we are blessed with an awakening comprehension as we begin to see that our "Father, and the Son, and the Holy Ghost are one" in the sense that they share a palpable divine power and authority.
(3 Nephi 11:27).

Baptism gives
our spiritual muscles
pliancy and flexibility,
and it softens our hearts
that had been cold and stony
to be receptive to the influence
of the Holy Ghost, which will
then make itself manifest
unto us according to
our faith.

Agency and opposition are powerful forces that constantly refine us by pushing, pulling, and tearing away at us within the crucible of experience. On our own, we cannot eliminate the consequences of sin. For that to happen, our Heavenly Father provided us with the Redeemer of Israel, Who can save us from our sins, thru repentance and baptism.

We are baptized that we might think less in terms of self sufficiency, and more about Christ dependency. We realize that His doctrine is intended to change not only behavior, but also nature.

As we respond to the
invitation to enter into the
fold, the Spirit moves upon us to
wash our flesh in water and to put
on holy garments, that we might
be prepared to enter into the
joy of the Lord.

Those who
are enamored with
themselves will never
experience the mind
and soul expanding
epiphany that they
are less than the
dust of the
earth.

If our hearts are hardened against the invitation to be baptized, it is as though our portion has been diminished further and further, until our natural defenses against the aggressive tactics of the Devil crumble, and we are left to fight our battles all by ourselves.

In the ordinance of baptism we make a solemn promise to serve God and to do His will. "No man can serve two masters: for either he will hate the one, and love the other; or else he will hold to the one, and despise the other." (Matthew 6:24). We cannot serve God when our hearts remain fixed upon the treasures of the earth.

When we are baptized, we
are very quickly introduced to the
pathway that leads to a Christ-centered
life. The Sacrament allows us to regularly
recommit ourselves to internalize every
truth relating to eternal progression,
and endows us with the capacity
to endure to the end in
righteousness.

"If ye will enter in by the way ... it will show unto you all things what ye should do. Behold, this is the doctrine of Christ."
(2 Nephi 32:5–6).

Following
our baptism, the
Holy Ghost teaches us
how we fit in to the divine
design of God. We learn how
faith can drive the law into
our inward parts. When it
does so, the articles of
our faith become the
particles of our
faith.

Whenever our priorities
are out of order, we lose the
power to bring about positive change.
Baptism, however, sharpens our perspective,
enabling us to comprehend and build
upon principles of perfection that
are validated by the Spirit and
emulated by the example
of the Savior.

The Gentile
nations of the earth
are to receive the Gospel,
and the elect among them are
to be converted by the power of
the Holy Ghost, to be baptized,
and to be carried along
the path leading to
eternal life.

Baptism creates
a groundswell of emotion that
generates the energy to lift us heavenward.
Worship is elevated to something that is more
dynamic than the simple mechanical observance
of a multiplicity of ceremonial rules. It helps
us to communicate feeling, capture emotion,
contour attitude, crystalize thought, congeal
passion, compartmentalize action, and
convey sentiments that creates
spiritual revitalization.

When we are baptized through God's infinite goodness, and the manifestations of the Spirit, we have great views of that which is to come. The soothing emanation of familiar oscillations of energy resonating from within the limitless reserves that are selflessly shared by the Holy Ghost carry us along on rolling waves of the Spirit toward a more sure personal witness of the Savior's divinity and of His sacrifice.

Heaven always holds its breath while waiting upon the initiative of those who have accepted the responsibility to provide a good example, and to take the lead when it comes to baptism.

The only payment required for the gift of salvation is the heart and a willing mind. The only things that we must give up are our sins.

If we find ourselves guilty of sustained spiritual neglect, drastic action will be necessary. The plastic surgery of repentance and baptism will be indicated if we hope to experience a reversal of our fortunes and if we are ever to reflect the likeness and image of God in our countenances.

Baptism, made possible by the Atonement, removes the stain of sin from the tapestry that is the tableau of our lives.

When we pass through the portal of baptism, our lives open up in an expansion of eternal opportunities as we obtain a remission of sins, gain membership in the Church, and are personally sanctified through the receipt of the Holy Ghost. We have the Spirit of God to be with us.

When we are baptized, the cobwebs in our minds are swept away, and we are blessed with the visitation of the Spirit which does nothing short of filling us with hope and perfect love.

Our progression hinges upon the the principles of the Atonement, repentance, baptism, and forgiveness, which just happen to be the polar opposites of life without light.

Paul painted a portrait of our second mile commitment thru baptism, when he wrote: "Ye are manifestly declared to be the epistle of Christ ministered by us, written not with ink, but with the Spirit of the living God; (and not just) in tables of stone, but (also) in fleshy tables of the heart." (2 Corinthians 3:3).

Our baptism allows us to make mistakes, to learn from them, and then to grasp the horns of sanctuary so that at the end of the day we may still be justified by the grace of God.

Those who
come to the
waters of baptism
are the pure in heart.
They enjoy the intrinsic
countermeasures to wicked
imaginations. Their behavior is
driven by altruism, self-denial,
self-discipline, self-restraint,
and self-sacrifice. These all
come as we listen with our
hearts to the promptings
of the Spirit that wash
over us as a gentle
breeze.

As fire in the sky,
the air in the theater of life
is charged with an electricity that
represents the inevitable merger of the
universal encouragement of the Light of
Christ with the guidance provided by the Holy
Ghost. Streaking in tandem across the heavens,
their trajectories coalesce to trace a flaming
trail that sparkles over a vast cosmic ocean
that is alive with energy. With the ebb and
flow of its tide, an effectual bridge of
understanding is thus created; one
that is buttressed by the cohesive
influence of the mighty
foundation of faith.

Raw and
ugly sores
that have been
inflicted by worldly
influences are healed
in the waters of baptism.
Its Balm of Gilead will
prevail over even the
most intimidating
onslaughts that
Babylon can
muster.

When agency
is exercised in an
atmosphere of opposition,
undesirable consequences will
sometimes follow. Their effects
can only be mitigated by
repentance and
baptism.

The characteristics of a Zion society are simply the result of a spiritual transformation that takes place in the lives of those who, after repentance, have been baptized and confirmed as members of The Church of Jesus Christ of Latter day Saints.

Our
baptism helps us to
be patient in our afflictions.
Knowing that the Lord is with us
until the end of our days helps us
to endure our trials and tribulations,
even when they are undeserved, or
we cannot understand why we
have been given them.
(See D&C 24:8).

When
we are under the
influence of the Spirit,
we speak of the doctrine in
a way that nurtures the faith
of those who are ready to take
their first step toward commitment
thru baptism, while, simultaneously,
more spiritually mature disciples, as
they realize that present levels of
performance are not acceptable,
are inspired to lengthen their
stride as they walk the
second mile of
faith.

"All those who humble themselves before God, and desire to be baptized (who) have truly repented of all their sins ... shall be received by baptism into his church." (D&C 20:37).

"Follow me, and do the things which ye have seen me do ... with full purpose of heart, acting no hypocrisy and no deception before God, but with real intent, repenting of your sins, witnessing unto the Father that ye are willing to take upon you the name of Christ by baptism."
(2 Nephi 3:12-13).

We
are baptized
so that, although
we were an hungered,
and thirsty, and strangers,
we will no longer be naked
or sick, or imprisoned within
the fortress of our own
limiting beliefs.

We are baptized because this life has been granted to us that we might prepare to meet our Heavenly Father on equal terms, in the sense that we can be holy and without spot. Baptism is the expression of our plea to the Savior to come to our rescue, and in particular to rely upon His Atonement to heal the damage of sin that has been inflicted upon us because of the weaknesses in our armor.

Recently baptized members of the Church qualify by worthiness to attend the temple where they may become as saviors on Mount Zion to their kindred dead. (See Obadiah 1:21). Work for our ancestors in the House of the Lord harmonizes perfectly with the doctrine that God is no respecter of persons, that He esteems all flesh as one, and that He views all of His children as living.

Following our baptism,
a dawn of recognition comes,
as we realize that we are the "elect
according to the foreknowledge of God
the Father, through sanctification of the
Spirit, unto obedience and sprinkling
of the blood of Jesus Christ."
(1 Peter 1:2).

Baptism nurtures us as we move from dependence, through independence, and then to the healthy and mature state of interdependence. It gives us the tools to enjoy unity and conformity, but without at the same time sacrificing what makes each of us unique.

When we do not repent, the Holy Spirit, which burns like a fire, will be quenched, and the Atonement will lose its power to save us from our sins, in baptism.

We are baptized
that we might honor
the priesthood, whose
performance requires the
authority of God, the blessing
and sanction of His file leaders,
exactness in its execution, and
the validation of witnesses.

We are baptized
to make it easier
for us to "pray unto
the Lord, (to) call upon
his holy name, (and to) make
known his wonderful works
among the people."
(D&C 65:4).

The Holy Ghost bears the most sacred witness of the validity of every Gospel ordinance. With the baptism of fire together with the unimpeachable witness of the Holy Ghost, the Atonement is complete, Mercy satisfies Justice, and the penitent faithful receive a remission of sins in a symbolic rite of purification.

We are baptized to become more observant followers of righteousness, to possess greater knowledge, to be the progenitors of nations and ambassadors of peace, and to receive instruction, and keep the commandments.

If we ignore
the law of baptism,
that is the only homing
beacon powerful enough to
penetrate the swirling mists of
darkness in our telestial world, we
will have tacitly chosen an alternate
course leading to destruction, as
our faith runs aground on the
rocky coastline of fear.

Baptism inspires
us to direct our charity
toward those who may deserve
it the least. It gently encourages
us to be humble and selfless,
and to be forbearing in
our own forgiveness
as we minister to
the needs of
others.

Baptism allows us to overcome our selfishness and our indefensible desire for Mercy without Justice. But this is nothing more than a doctrine of the devil.

Baptism
means forsaking
the carnal nature
that is nothing more
than a shadowy after
image of Lucifer's
rebellion at the
Council.

The insolvency
of Satan's seduction
cannot be mitigated by
a third-party bailout. The
only resolution of his
malevolent nepotism
is to repent and
be baptized.

The Devil urges us to follow a detour from the strait and narrow way that leads us to doctrinal dead-ends, religious roundabouts and conceptual cul de sacs; and thru telestial traffic, from which the only escape possible is baptism by immersion.

It is nothing short of sin that motivates us to drag our battered and beaten bodies to the baptismal font.

# About The Author

Phil Hudson and his wife Jan have 7 children and over 25 grandchildren. They enjoy spending time with their family at their cabin nestled in the Selkirk Mountains, on the shore of Priest Lake, the crown jewel of North Idaho. Phil had a successful dental practice in Spokane, Washington for 43 years, before retiring in 2015. He has an eclectic mix of hobbies, and enjoys the out of doors. He always finds time, however, to record his thoughts on his laptop, and understands Isaac Asimov's response when he was asked: If you knew that you had only 10 minutes left to live, what would you do?" He answered: "I'd type faster."

Phil received the inspiration to write this book while he and Jan were serving as missionaries for The Church of Jesus Christ of Latter-day Saints, in the Kingdom of Tonga. While there, they celebrated their 50th wedding anniversary.

Our innate desire to be clean will find expression in the celestial sparks that ignite our desire to repent and be baptized.

# By The Author

Essays

    Volume One: Spray From The Ocean Of Thought
    Volume Two: Ripples On A Pond
    Volume Three: Serendipitous Meanderings
    Volume Four: Presents Of Mind
    Volume Five: Mental Floss
    Volume Six: Fitness Training For The Mind And Spirit

First Principles and Ordinances Series

    Faith – Our Hearts Are Changed
    Repentance – A Broken Heart and a Contrite Spirit
    Baptism – One Hundred And One Reasons Why We Are Baptized
    The Holy Ghost – That We Might Have His Spirit To Be With Us
    The Sacrament – This Do In Remembrance Of Me

Book of Mormon Commentary

    Volume One: Born In The Wilderness
    Volume Two: Voices From The Dust
    Volume Three: Journey To Cumorah

Doctrine & Covenants Commentary

- Volume One - Sections 1 - 34
- Volume Two - Sections 35 - 57

Minute Musings: Spontaneous Combustions of Thought

- Volume One
- Volume Two
- Volume Three

Calendars:

- In His Own Words: Discovering William Tyndale
- As I Think About The Savior
- Scriptural Symbols

Children's Books

- Muddy, Muddy
- The Thirteen Articles of Faith
- Happy Birthday

Doctrinal Themes

    The House of the Lord

A Thought For Each Day of the Year

    Faith
    Repentance
    Baptism
    The Holy Ghost
    The Sacrament
    The House of the Lord
    The Plan of Salvation
    The Atonement
    Revelation

Professional Publications

    Diode Laser Soft Tissue Surgery Volume One
    Diode Laser Soft Tissue Surgery Volume Two
    Diode Laser Soft Tissue Surgery Volume Three

These, and other titles, are available from online retailers.

As
long as we
remain in a state
of rebellion against the
Spirit, the fruit of the Tree
of Life will remain just beyond
our reach, even if out of curiosity,
we now and then attempt to take a
bite. If we never raise our eyes to
search eternal horizons, the world
before us will appear as nothing
more than a barren desert that
is devoid of refreshing oases,
the welcome shade of trees,
and an abundance of well
watered gardens. If we
lack enough faith to
be baptized for a
remission of our
sins, its living
water cannot
sustain us.
us.

Quid magis possum dicere?

www.ingramcontent.com/pod-product-compliance
Lightning Source LLC
Chambersburg PA
CBHW060507240426
43661CB00007B/947